Be My Valentine

I Talk You Talk Press

CONTENTS

1. THESE ARE FOR YOU

Oscar Beadon is a very handsome man. He has a good job, and a lot of money. He drives a sports car. He dates many girls. They are always beautiful. Sometimes the girls fall in love with Oscar, but he never falls in love with them. He doesn't want to fall in love. He doesn't want to get married. He enjoys his single life. He dates a girl for about six weeks, then he drops her, and finds a new girlfriend. He makes many women very unhappy, but he doesn't care.

Then something very surprising happens. Oscar falls in love. It happens like this.

When Oscar meets a new girl, he buys them presents. The girls are very happy. They think that Oscar likes them a lot. There is a flower shop two streets away from his office. Oscar goes there to buy flowers. Near the flower shop is a small café. It has tables outside. Many people sit outside, drinking coffee, and watching the street.

One day, Oscar is walking past the café, when he sees a girl. She is the new waitress at the café. She is the most beautiful girl Oscar has ever seen. Oscar goes past the café to the flower shop. He buys an orchid to give to his latest girlfriend. Her name is Belle. She is a model. That night, Oscar takes Belle to an expensive restaurant. Belle is very famous, so everyone looks at her. Oscar should feel proud, but he doesn't. All he can think about is the new waitress at the café.

I must be very careful, thinks Oscar. *I must stop thinking about that waitress. I don't want to have a serious girlfriend.*

But it's no good. All the next week, Oscar thinks about the waitress day and night.

Don't be stupid, he tells himself. *Your girlfriends are always actresses or*

1

models. You don't date waitresses from cafes. You don't even know her name!

Oscar stays away from the street where the flower shop and café are. He doesn't want to see the beautiful girl.

That would be dangerous, he thinks.

Belle calls Oscar every day. She wonders why Oscar hasn't called her, or asked her out on another date.

Oscar says, "I'm sorry. I'm very busy at work. I'll call you soon."

On February 13, Belle calls Oscar again. "Tomorrow is Valentine's Day. There's a big party at the new five-star hotel in the centre of the city. Would you like to come with me? There will be a lot of very famous and interesting people there."

"Thank you Belle. But I don't think so," says Oscar. "I will be busy tomorrow."

"You have another girlfriend don't you!" shouts Belle. She is very angry. "Five different men have asked me out on a date tomorrow night. I will go out with one of those! Don't ever call me again!"

Oscar doesn't care. He doesn't want to see Belle any more. He wants to talk to the beautiful girl at the café.

It doesn't matter that she is a waitress. She is so beautiful. I think I am in love with her. Tomorrow I will go to the café and ask her out on a date. She will be my new girlfriend.

Oscar never thinks that the waitress will say 'no'. Women always say 'yes' when Oscar asks them to go out with him.

The next day, he goes to the flower shop and buys twelve red roses.

The woman in the flower shop knows Oscar well. He is one of her best customers.

"This is the first time you have bought roses," she says.

"Usually I don't buy roses," says Oscar. "They are too romantic."

"Then this girl must be special," says the woman.

"Oh, she is," says Oscar. "She is very special."

Oscar pays for the roses. They are beautiful. Then he goes to the café. He will give them to the waitress. He is sure that he is in love with her. He is sure that she will love him too.

Oscar gets a shock when he gets to the café. The girl is not there! An older woman is serving tables. "Uh, excuse me," he says to her. "Where is the usual waitress?"

"Anita?" answers the woman. "It's her lunch break. She usually goes and sits in the park."

"Which park?" asks Oscar.

"I don't know the name, but it's about half a kilometre from here. Straight down the road. It's next to the church."

"Oh, yes. I know it. Thank you," says Oscar.

Oscar hurries to the park. It's a big park with a lake, and a play area for children. He looks everywhere for Anita. Then he sees her. She is standing near the lake. He hurries towards her, carrying the roses. Then he sees that she is with a young man. The man has his arms around her. Oscar watches as Anita looks up at the man. She puts her hand on his face. They are talking softly.

Oscar feels very bad. *Oh no! She loves someone else! She doesn't know that I love her. She doesn't even know who I am. I am an idiot!*

Oscar walks away very quickly. He walks towards the park gates. He is very unhappy, and he feels stupid. He doesn't look where he is walking. He bangs into a woman. She drops her bag on the ground.

"Sorry," he says. He bends down to pick up the bag, and hands it back to her.

The woman smiles. "Thank you," she says. Then she looks at him. "Are you OK? You look like you had a shock."

The woman is very old. Her clothes are old. Oscar thinks she is poor. He is still holding the roses.

"I'm fine," he says. He gives the roses to the old woman. "These are for you."

He turns and walks away.

When he is back on the street, he calls Belle. "I have finished work, and so I'm free tonight. Do you still want me to take you to the party at the hotel?"

Belle already has a date. But Oscar is more handsome and he has more money. *I'll cancel my date and go with Oscar,* she thinks.

Anita is still by the lake. She is saying goodbye to her brother, Gino.

"I will worry about you so much!" she says. "Please be careful in Africa."

"I'll be careful," says Gino. "And you be careful too. I'll miss you. I wish you had a boyfriend to look after you."

Anita laughs. "I don't need a boyfriend."

"Isn't there anyone you like?" asks Gino.

"Yes, there is. He's very handsome. He often goes to the flower shop near the café. But he doesn't know me. He doesn't even know my name, and I don't know his."

The old woman is in the churchyard. She is sitting next to a gravestone. The gravestone reads:

---Walter Jones, Born: September 2nd, 1929. Died: February 14th, 1999---

She takes some dead flowers from a vase in front of the gravestone.

"I didn't have enough money to buy flowers for you today," she says.

She puts the red roses into the vase. "But God is good. He sent a man with these flowers. Happy Valentine's Day, Walter. These are for you."

2. THE PROPOSAL

Simon and Kate have been dating for two years. They met in their last year at university. Simon works in a bank. Kate is a kindergarten teacher. When Simon goes back to work after the Christmas holiday, his boss says, "I have great news for you! The bank is transferring you to Wallaceville! It's a bigger branch, and you'll get a salary increase. It will be good experience for you."

"Oh, thank you," says Simon. "When will I start there?"

"At the beginning of March," says his boss.

In fact, Simon is not very happy. He knows that it is a great chance for him, but Wallaceville is 150km away. He will have to move there. He doesn't want to leave Kate. He loves Kate very much.

I want to marry Kate. I want her to come to Wallaceville with me. I will ask her to marry me. But will she say 'yes'? I don't know if she loves me as much as I love her, and she likes her job at the kindergarten. Maybe she will say 'no'.

Simon feels very nervous, but he knows he must be brave. He will propose to Kate.

It must be the perfect proposal, he thinks. *I must make a good plan. But first I have to buy a ring.*

Simon buys a beautiful diamond ring. It is very expensive.

Now I'll make a plan. When, and where shall I ask her to marry me? he asks himself.

'When' is easy.

I will propose to Kate on Valentine's Day. It's the perfect day. But where? I have spent almost all my savings on the ring. I can't take Kate to a nice restaurant. I'll ask Kate to come to my apartment. I'll cook something delicious for dinner. I will buy a bottle of champagne. We can watch a romantic movie together, and then I'll ask her to marry me.

Simon is pleased with his plan. He invites Kate to come to his apartment for dinner on February 14. Simon is not a great cook, but he can cook pasta. The day before Valentine's Day he buys the ingredients for a cream and prawn sauce to serve with the pasta. He thinks Kate will like it. He buys one very beautiful big chocolate. He cuts the bottom out of the chocolate and puts the ring inside. He will serve it to Kate for dessert. He buys champagne and rents the DVD of *Roman Holiday*. It's a very old movie, but Simon thinks Kate looks like Audrey Hepburn.

Simon hurries home from work on Valentine's Day. He puts *Roman Holiday* in the DVD player. He makes the pasta sauce. He puts a cloth and plates and glasses on the table. He puts a small plate with the chocolate on it in the center of the table.

The doorbell is ringing. Kate has arrived! Simon runs to answer the door.

Kate looks as beautiful as always, but she also looks very tired.

"I'm so pleased we're not going out tonight," she says. "A quiet evening watching television is just what I need. I had a very busy day at work."

"Sit down and relax," says Simon. "I'll go and get the food ready."

"Thank you," smiles Kate.

Simon leaves Kate in the living room and goes to the kitchen. He cooks the pasta and heats the sauce. He opens the champagne. He takes the food and wine back to the living room. Kate is not sitting at the table. She's on the sofa and she's asleep!

Simon doesn't know whether to wake her up or not. She looks so cute. *And she was so tired,* he thinks. *I will leave her to sleep.*

Simon sits at the table and waits for Kate to wake up. He waits and waits. The pasta gets cold. He takes it out to the kitchen and puts it in the refrigerator. He reads the newspaper. He makes some toast and eats it. Kate is still sleeping.

Simon gives up. He finds a blanket and covers Kate so she won't get cold. He goes to bed feeling very disappointed.

My plan was no good, he thinks. *We didn't eat the food I cooked. We didn't drink the champagne. We didn't watch Roman Holiday together. I didn't propose. What a terrible Valentine's Day!*

Simon is falling asleep when he hears a loud sound from the living room.

"Ow!" Kate shouts. He runs to the living room. Kate is standing next to the table. Her mouth is bleeding.

"Kate! Kate! What happened?" asks Simon.

"Oh, Simon, I'm so sorry. You cooked food for us, but I fell asleep. I didn't eat anything. Then when I woke up, I was so hungry. There was a chocolate on the table. I tried to eat it. But there was something sharp inside the chocolate. My mouth is cut."

Simon finds a towel. He brings ice from the kitchen. Finally, Kate's mouth stops bleeding.

"Uh, Kate."

"Yes, Simon?"

"Did you eat all the chocolate?"

"No. I dropped it when it cut my mouth. It must be on the floor."

Simon looks at the floor. He can't see the ring. He crawls around looking for it.

Kate is surprised. "What are you doing?" she asks.

"I have to find the chocolate," says Simon.

"Maybe it's under the sofa," says Kate.

Simon looks under the sofa. It's very dusty underneath. The half-eaten chocolate is lying there.

"You should take that chocolate back to the shop," says Kate. "They should give you your money back. There must have been glass in it."

"No. It wasn't glass," says Simon. "It was something for you."

He gives the dusty chocolate to Kate. She looks at it.

"What's this?" she asks.

"It's an engagement ring," says Simon. "It was a stupid idea. I put the ring in the chocolate. I'm sorry. I was going to ask you to marry me tonight, but everything went wrong."

Kate laughs. "I'm sorry too. I went to sleep, and you couldn't propose."

Kate and Simon sit on the sofa. Simon pours some champagne. It has no bubbles left, and it's warm, but it doesn't matter.

"It wasn't a good Valentine's Day," says Kate. "But just think. It will make a wonderful story to tell everyone at our wedding!"

"Does that mean you will marry me?" says Simon.

"Of course," says Kate. She takes a fork from the table and pulls the ring out of the chocolate. She puts it on her finger. It's covered in chocolate and very sticky, but she doesn't care. Simon is very happy. "My plan went wrong, but this is the best Valentine's Day ever!"

3. THE BEST WHITE DAY PRESENT EVER

Takuma Kato opened his eyes and looked at the clock.

Seven forty-five! Oh no! I've overslept! I'm going to be late for work! he thought. He jumped out of bed and quickly got dressed.

He hurried into the bathroom to wash his face and brush his teeth.

I'll get some breakfast at the convenience store on the way to work, he thought. *I've no time to make anything.*

He put his shoes on and left his apartment. He ran down the stairs and across the car park. He didn't stop running until he got to the train station. Luckily a train came almost immediately.

On the train, Takuma looked around at the other businessmen.

That's strange, he thought. *Many of the men are carrying gift bags. Most of the bags are from the nice cookie shop in the department store near the station.*

Then, he remembered. He took his smartphone out of his pocket and checked the date.

March 14th! It's White Day! And I don't have any cookies! Oh no!

Takuma worked in a small office in Kagoshima City. He was the only man in his office. His boss, and his four colleagues, were all women. He got on well with the women in his office, and they all liked him very much.

On February 14, Valentine's Day, all the women in the office gave Takuma chocolates. Takuma loved chocolate, so he always looked forward to Valentine's Day. In Japan, women give chocolates to men on Valentine's Day. Many women buy chocolates for their male work colleagues. Then, on March 14, which is called 'White Day' in Japan, the men buy cookies or other sweets for the women in return.

In early March, Takuma had been very busy at work. He had been on a three-day business trip in Fukuoka until the day before. When he came back to Kagoshima, he had to write a report about his trip. He only finished it at 1:00am that morning.

I completely forgot about White Day! he thought. *I buy the ladies in the office nice cookies every White Day. They will be disappointed if I don't have any this year. I'll have to buy some White Day cookies in the convenience store. They won't be as nice as the cookies I buy every year at the department store, but they are better than nothing.*

The train arrived at the station, and Takuma hurried out of the station and into the convenience store. He saw one box of White Day cookies near the counter.

There's only one box of cookies left! he thought. He hurried to the cookies, but there was another businessman in front of him. The other businessman picked up the box of cookies and took it to the cash register.

Oh no! I'm three seconds too late! thought Takuma. He looked around the convenience store. There were normal cookies, chocolates and sweets, but they didn't look very special.

The ladies in the office expect nice White Day cookies, he thought. *I can't buy them cheap, normal cookies. Maybe I can buy something on my lunch break.*

Takuma bought an egg sandwich and a can of black coffee and hurried to the office. He arrived at 8:30, just in time for work.

"Good morning!" said Keiko, the building receptionist. "It's a nice day isn't it? Spring has come at last!"

"Good morning!" said Takuma as he hurried to the elevator. "Yes, it's a lovely day."

Takuma hadn't noticed the blue sky and gentle spring breeze outside. He walked into the office.

"Good morning, Kato san," said Chiharu Yamasaki.

"Good morning, Yamasaki san," said Takuma. *Oh no! She's looking at my hands. She's looking for cookies!* he thought.

He said hello to everyone in the office, and sat down at his desk.

They must think I've forgotten White Day, he thought. *Should I say something? No, I can't say that I forgot. I'll buy something special for them in the department store at lunch time.*

It was a very busy morning for Takuma. He had a lot of work to do. He soon forgot about White Day and the cookies.

"Kato san."

Chiharu was standing next to Takuma. She was starting to get worried about him.

"Kato san," she said again.

"Oh!" Takuma looked up at her. "Sorry, I didn't hear you," he said.

"Aren't you going to have lunch today?" she asked.

"Why? What time is it?" asked Takuma.

"Three thirty."

"Three thirty! I didn't realise it was so late!"

"I think you should take a break," said Chiharu. "You've been working at your computer since you came in this morning. Your eyes must be tired. And I'm sure you're hungry. I can hear your stomach rumbling."

Takuma rubbed his eyes. "Yes, I am quite hungry. I'll go for lunch now," he said. He put his coat on and walked out of the office.

Chiharu waited until Takuma had gone and turned to Sachiko.

"Do you think he has forgotten that it's White Day?" she asked.

"It looks like it. He always brings us cookies on White Day," said Sachiko.

"Yeah, and they are always those really nice cookies from the department store," said Emi, walking over to Chiharu's desk.

"Maybe that's where he's gone," said Chiharu. "He might come back with the cookies. He was nearly late for work this morning. He must have overslept. So he didn't have time to buy any."

"He had the business trip to Fukuoka, then he had to write up the report, so he has been very busy recently," said Sachiko.

"That's true," said Emi. "Never mind! If he doesn't come back with any cookies, I guess we will just have to wait until next year!"

Chiharu nodded. "I guess so," she said.

Takuma walked into the department store. He hurried over to the cookie shop.

"Excuse me," he said to the girl behind the counter. "Do you have any of those white chocolate cookies left?"

"The ones in the cute pink boxes?" asked the girl. "I'm sorry. We've sold out. These are the only White Day cookies we have left."

She pointed to three small bags of cookies.

There are only three bags! thought Takuma. *I need five!*

"OK, thank you," he said. He walked out of the department store and went to a ramen shop. He ordered a large bowl of hot noodles and sat in a corner alone.

I'll have to say sorry to the ladies in the office when I go back, he thought.

Just then, many people in the noodle shop started to talk loudly. Takuma looked up. Jiro, a local singer, had come into the shop. Jiro was famous in Takuma's town. He started his singing career by singing and playing the guitar outside the station. He had been in Takuma's older brother's class at school, so Takuma knew him a little.

It's Jiro! All the ladies in the office like him, thought Takuma. *He has a concert at the end of the month. Chiharu was talking about it last week.*

Jiro sat down at the counter and talked to the shop owner while he waited for his noodles.

Then, Takuma had a great idea.

He finished his noodles and walked over to Jiro.

"Excuse me," he said.

Jiro turned around.

"I'm sorry to disturb you. I'm Takuma Kato, Takeshi's brother. You were in Takeshi's class at school," said Takuma.

Jiro looked at him for a few seconds, then he smiled.

"Yeah, that's right! You're Takeshi's little brother! I remember you! How is Takeshi? What's he doing now?"

"He's fine. He's working for a bank in Singapore. He's been there for a few years," said Takuma.

"Really? That's cool," said Jiro. "I'd love to go to Singapore. Next time you speak to him, tell him I said 'hi'. Tell him I want to visit Singapore someday."

"I will. Thanks. Jiro, I wonder if I could ask you a favour. Do you have ten minutes free when you have finished your noodles?"

"Sure. I don't have any plans after this. Why?"

Takuma and Jiro talked for a few minutes, then Takuma went back to the office with a smile on his face.

Twenty minutes later, Keiko called Takuma's office. He answered the phone.

"Kato speaking," he said.

"There's a visitor here to see you," said Keiko.

Takuma smiled. Keiko seemed very excited.

"Who is it?"

"It's Jiro!" she said quietly. "The singer!"

"Send him up please," said Takuma. He watched the door and waited. A few seconds later, Jiro walked into the office. Takuma looked at his colleagues. They all looked very surprised.

"It's Jiro!" whispered Sachiko to Emi. "I don't believe it!"

"Wow! What is he doing here?" whispered Chiharu.

Takuma walked over to Jiro and they started to talk.

"How does Takuma know him?" whispered Emi.

"His brother was in the same class at school," whispered Chiharu.

"Do you think we can ask him for his autograph, and a photo?" whispered Sachiko.

Then, Jiro and Takuma walked over to them.

"Ladies, I'd like to introduce you to Jiro," said Takuma.

Everyone was very excited. They all used their smartphones to take photographs of each other with Jiro. Chiharu asked him to sign her diary. Sachiko asked him to sign her pencil case.

"And ladies, because it's White Day, I have a surprise for you," said Jiro.

He took some tickets out of his pocket.

"VIP tickets to my concert at the end of the month. You will have front row seats, and you can come backstage after the concert to meet my band members," said Jiro, handing out the tickets.

Everyone started laughing and clapping. Takuma watched them and smiled.

Jiro and Takuma walked out to the elevator.

"Thank you so much Jiro," said Takuma.

"It's a pleasure," said Jiro. "I'm always pleased if I can make people happy."

"You certainly made the ladies happy," said Takuma. "And you helped me, too!"

"And you made me happy too. I don't have much money, so I haven't been able to go on any trips abroad. But if I can stay at Takeshi's apartment, I only need to pay for my flight to Singapore. Tell Takeshi I'm looking forward to staying with him in summer!"

"I will," said Takuma. Jiro got in the elevator and the doors closed.

I'll talk to Takeshi tomorrow. I hope he doesn't mind Jiro staying with him for a few days, thought Takuma.

He went back into the office. The women were still talking about Jiro's visit.

"Kato san, this is the best White Day present ever! Thank you so much!" said Chiharu.

"Yes, it's better than cookies! A lot better than cookies!" said

Sachiko.

"We thought you had forgotten it was White Day!" said Emi.

Takuma smiled. "Of course I didn't forget!" he said. "Of course not!"

4. WHO IS IT FROM?

Stacey and Rebecca were sitting in the university library. They were studying hard for their exams. Rebecca checked the time on her smartphone.

"Stacey, it's eleven o'clock. We've been studying for three hours. Shall we take a break?"

Stacey yawned. "Good idea."

They stood up and walked to the entrance of the library. "We're just going for a break," said Rebecca. "We've left our bags and books on the large table over there."

The librarian, Eric Biggins, looked up from his computer and smiled.

"OK," he said. "Thank you for letting me know."

Stacey and Rebecca walked out of the library, and went down the stairs to the cafeteria. They bought cans of cola from the vending machine, and sat down at a free table.

"It is Valentine's Day tomorrow," said Rebecca. "Are you sending anyone a Valentine's Day card?"

"No, not this year. I can't think of anything but this exam. Are you?"

"No, there's no one in my classes that I like. I used to send lots of cards to boys I liked in high school," said Rebecca.

"Did you write your name on them?" asked Stacey.

"Of course not. I wrote a message and signed the cards with a question mark. 'From ?' Of course, I think some people knew it was me who sent them. They knew my handwriting."

"I did that too," said Stacey. "But I think I'm too old to do that now. Only kids do that."

"That's true. But it was fun though, wasn't it?" said Rebecca. "People always looked so happy when they got cards. They would look around the class all day, thinking 'Who sent me the card?' I used to enjoy seeing their faces."

"Yeah, it was fun," said Stacey.

They finished their drinks and walked back up to the library.

"We're back," said Rebecca to Eric.

He looked up from his computer and smiled. "OK," he said.

They sat down, and opened their books again.

"Stacey," whispered Rebecca. "Do you think Mr Biggins has ever received a Valentine's Day card?"

"Probably not."

"How old do you think he is?" asked Rebecca.

"About fifty? He's still single though. I heard that he still lives with his mother. Why?"

"Why don't we send him a Valentine's Day card? I think it will make him very happy."

Stacey smiled. "That's a good idea. But we have to hurry. Valentine's Day is tomorrow."

"Let's buy a card after our lunch break," said Rebecca.

Two hours later, Stacey and Rebecca were in the post office. Rebecca wrote in the card: *---Dear Eric, Happy Valentine's Day, love from ?---*

"Perfect," said Stacey. She wrote the address of the university library on the envelope, and took it to the counter.

"I'd like to send this by express post please," she said.

They paid and walked out of the post office.

"I hope he likes his surprise!" said Rebecca.

The next day, Eric Biggins went down to the university office to pick up the post for the library.

"Good morning Eric," said Sandra.

"Good morning Sandra," said Eric. "Is there any post for the library today?"

Sandra smiled. "There is one letter. Here." She passed him a red envelope.

Eric looked at it. "A red envelope? And it's addressed to me personally. What is it?"

"It's Valentine's Day today. Maybe it's a Valentine's Day card," said Sandra.

Eric felt very embarrassed. "Oh, er…oh. Right, er…is there anything else?"

"No, just that," said Sandra.

Eric walked out of the office and hurried back up the stairs. He sat behind the library counter and opened the card.

---*Dear Eric, Happy Valentine's Day, love from ?*---

A Valentine's Day card for me! he thought. *But who is it from?*

The first students of the day started to come into the library. Eric put the card back in the envelope and put it in his bag. Ten minutes later, Stacey and Rebecca walked into the library.

"Good morning!" said Eric. "How is everyone today? Lovely day, isn't it?"

"Yes, it is. How are you today Mr Biggins?" asked Stacey.

"I'm very well, thank you! I'm marvellous!" said Eric.

Rebecca and Stacey smiled. They sat down in a corner.

"That card made him so happy!" whispered Stacey. "It was a great idea!"

Eric couldn't concentrate on his work that day. He could only think about the card.

Who sent it? he thought. *Was it Sandra? No, she's married. Was it…could it be…was it Sue? No…but…*

Eric liked Sue. She had been working in the office for many years. She was forty-seven, and divorced.

When no one was looking, Eric sat down and took the card out of his bag. He looked carefully at the writing on the envelope. *It looks like Sue's writing! The 'g' and the 'y' look like Sue's! I'm sure it's Sue. Does this mean she likes me? Maybe this is my chance!* he thought.

Eric spent all day thinking. By the end of the day, he had made a plan.

The next morning, Eric went to work early, and waited in his car for Sue to arrive. Soon, he saw her car come into the car park.

He got out of the car and locked the door. His legs were shaking. *I have to be brave. I have to be brave,* he thought.

Sue got out of her car.

"Good morning Eric," she said.

"Good morning. Er, Sue, I was wondering…would you like to go for lunch today?" asked Eric.

Sue looked very surprised.

"Lunch?"

"Yes," said Eric. His voice was shaking.

"Yes, I'd like to go for lunch with you. That would be lovely, Eric. Thank you," said Sue.

"Really? You'd like to go?" asked Eric. He couldn't believe it.

"Yes, of course! We could go to that tearoom near the station."

And so it started. Before long, Eric and Sue started dating.

In August, they went to the seaside for a summer holiday. One day, they were sitting on the beach. Sue was reading and Eric was looking at the sea. He was thinking about his life.

That Valentine's Day card changed everything, he thought. He looked at Sue.

"Sue, I'm so glad you sent me that Valentine's Day card. If you hadn't sent it, we wouldn't be a couple. I had no idea that you liked me," said Eric.

Sue looked up from her book and looked at Eric.

"What Valentine's Day card?" asked Sue.

"The Valentine's Day card!" said Eric.

"But Eric, I didn't send you a Valentine's Day card!"

"What? But someone sent me a card! I thought it was you!"

"I didn't send it."

"You didn't send it?" Eric couldn't believe it.

"No. So another woman likes you! I'm very lucky to have you, Eric. It seems you are quite popular!" said Sue.

"I had the courage to ask you to lunch that day, because I thought you had sent the card," said Eric. "I don't know who sent it, but I'm glad they did."

"I'm glad they sent it too!" said Sue. "But I hope they don't send you one next year. I wouldn't be happy with that!"

5. WE WANT OUR COOKIES

Rosetta Wilcox teaches the kindergarten class at the local elementary school. On Valentine's Day last year, she made cookies for the children in her class. She had eighteen students. She made eighteen big cookies and decorated them. She wrote the name of each child on their cookie with sugar icing.

Rosetta took the cookies to school.

"We have a treat for lunchtime today," she told the children. "I have a cookie for everyone."

"Can we have our cookies now?" asked Robbie.

"No. You must wait until lunchtime. After you have eaten your school lunch, you can eat your cookies."

The children were excited.

"I'm going to eat all my cookie in one big bite," said Wallace.

"I'm going to save mine," said Angela. "I'm going to take it home and show my mother."

"No! Eat it!" shouted Felicity. "Eat it after lunch!"

The children were making a lot of noise. Rosetta laughed. "They are only cookies! They are not so special."

There was a knock at the door.

"Quiet please, children," said Rosetta. "We have a visitor."

Rosetta went to the door and opened it.

The head teacher of the elementary school, Mrs Stringer, was standing there. Next to her, was a very small boy.

"This is Teddy. He is going to join your class. Teddy, this is Miss Wilcox. She will be your new teacher," said Mrs Stringer.

"Hello, Teddy," said Rosetta. "Welcome."

Teddy looked at the floor. He didn't smile. Rosetta thought he looked very sad.

"Come in, Teddy," said Rosetta. Teddy walked into the room.

"Robbie," said Rosetta. "Teddy will sit next to you. Please come and show him his seat."

Robbie jumped up and took Teddy's hand. "Here. You will sit next to me. My seat is the best seat, but you can have the one next to me."

Mrs Stringer spoke very quickly and quietly to Rosetta.

"Poor little boy. His parents were killed in a car crash only a week ago. His only family now is his grandmother. There was some family trouble and he had never met her. She went to New York to bring him back here. She is a good kind woman, but he is so sad and lonely. His grandmother thought he might do better if he came to school and made some friends."

"Oh, dear," said Rosetta. "I will do my best."

"Now, Teddy," said Mrs Stringer. "Please come with me. I will give you a tour of the school, so that you know where everything is. Then we'll go and see the school nurse."

Teddy got up and walked out the room with Mrs Stringer.

"Now, everyone, find your reading books," said Rosetta. "We will have reading until lunchtime."

"Then cookies!" shouted Wallace.

"Cookies, cookies," the other children shouted.

Oh, no! thought Rosetta. *What am I going to do? I don't have a cookie for Teddy. He will feel bad if all the other children have cookies. I am sure the children will understand. They must be kind to the new boy. I will tell them they can't have cookies today.*

Just before lunchtime, Rosetta spoke to the children.

"I have your cookies here. But we have a new class member. He will be here at lunchtime, or soon after. I don't have a cookie for him. He will feel bad, and we want to make him feel welcome."

The children stared at Rosetta. They didn't say anything.

"So, we will have the cookies tomorrow! I will make a cookie for Teddy tonight."

"No!" "Today is Valentine's Day." "You promised!" "I want my cookie now!"

"Quiet!" shouted Rosetta.

The children were quiet.

"You must be nice to new people. I want you to wait until tomorrow," said Rosetta.

"I don't care about the new boy." "It's not fair. Why can't we have our cookies?" "I hate the new boy!"

All the children were talking at once.

"OK!" Rosetta shouted again. "It's true. I promised you the cookies. So you can have them. But I hoped you would think about the new boy."

The children were all smiling. Rosetta gave them each the cookie with their name on it. Then she took the children down to the cafeteria. She waited until the children had their meals and were sitting down. Then she went to the teachers' room to eat her sandwiches. Mrs Stringer was there, drinking coffee and reading a magazine.

"Where's the new boy, Teddy?" asked Rosetta.

"He is with the school nurse. She wants to check him because he has no medical records here. She'll take him to the cafeteria."

Rosetta sat down and sighed. "What's wrong?" asked Mrs Stringer. "You look tired."

"No, I'm not tired. But I am very disappointed with my class. They are very selfish. I don't think they are nice children."

Mrs Stringer laughed. "They are young children. Of course, they are sometimes selfish."

"But I thought I had taught them to think about other people!"

"Don't worry about it. I am sure they are very nice children. But people aren't perfect all the time!"

Rosetta ate her sandwiches and drank a cup of coffee. Then she went back to the cafeteria to take the children back to their classroom. But they weren't there!

"Where is my class?" she asked one of the staff.

"They left early," the woman answered. "The school nurse came with a small boy. When the nurse went away, all the children stood up and left. They took the little boy with them. I think they went outside."

Oh no! What are they doing? Rosetta was in a panic. She ran out of the cafeteria and outside into the playground. The children were standing in a circle. *They might be bullying him,* she thought. *This is terrible!*

The children didn't notice Rosetta. She hurried towards them. Angela was talking.

"Today is Valentine's Day. Miss Wilcox made cookies for us. She made one cookie for everyone. But there's no cookie for you, because you are the new boy. We don't know you."

Rosetta felt sick. *My students are so unkind!* she thought.

Then Wallace said, "So we are giving you some of our cookies."

Felicity had a plate. On the plate were pieces of cookie. "We all broke our cookies up. So you have a piece of eighteen cookies. Here you are."

"Miss Wilcox said we have to say 'welcome'," said Robbie.

Then all the children together said, "Welcome."

Rosetta's eyes were full of tears. *They are nice children. They have learned to care about other people,* she thought.

Wallace saw Rosetta. "Hey! Miss Wilcox! We are welcoming Teddy!"

"Yes you are, children," said Rosetta. "That is very nice. And now we must go back to our classroom."

The children moved towards her and Rosetta saw Teddy. He was holding the plate and he was smiling.

6. NO PETS

The cat followed Tanya home from the restaurant. It was very thin and dirty. Tanya tried to ignore it, but it didn't go away.

"Shoo!" said Tanya to the cat. "Why are you following me?"

When Tanya got to her apartment building, the cat was still there. Her apartment was on the second floor. The cat followed her up the stairs.

"Go away!"

The cat didn't take any notice. It sat on the mat in front of Tanya's door and waited for her to find her key, and unlock the door.

"You can't come in," said Tanya. "I'm not allowed pets."

Tanya opened the door and went into her apartment. She closed the door with the cat outside. She felt very bad but she couldn't let the cat inside. The cat started scratching on the door and making strange little sounds.

I mustn't listen, thought Tanya. *It was very difficult to find this apartment. It's cheap and convenient. If the owner finds out that I let a cat inside, he will tell me to go. But I feel terrible. The cat sounds like it's crying, and it's so thin and dirty.*

Tanya took off her heavy coat and boots. She left them in the front hallway. The apartment was very cold. She turned on the gas heater in the tiny living room and then went to the kitchen. She shut the door. *Maybe if I ignore it, the cat will go away,* she thought.

Tanya was working in an Italian restaurant. She wanted to be a chef. She went to cooking school, but now it was winter vacation, and Tanya had got a job in the restaurant to get some experience.

The chef at the restaurant knew that Tanya was a student. She knew that Tanya didn't have much money, so she often gave her food that was left over. Tanya opened her bag and took out the food containers. Today she had vegetable soup, two meatballs and some salmon. Tanya was hungry. She put the soup in a pot, and put it on the gas burner to heat up.

Then the doorbell rang. Tanya turned the gas off and went to the door. She looked through the spyhole. It was a courier deliveryman.

She opened the door. The man handed her a parcel and she signed the form. She took the parcel back to the kitchen. She didn't notice that the cat had come in.

The parcel was from her mother. It was long woollen underwear. Tanya read her mother's note.

---*You must be so cold. I wish you would come home for the holidays. We miss you.*---

Tanya's eyes filled with tears. She was very lonely, living alone in a big city. She wanted to go home, but getting her chef's diploma was important too.

Something rubbed against Tanya's legs.

"What…?" she screamed. She looked down. It was the cat.

"How did you get in?" she asked. "Oh, of course, you ran in when I opened the door for the deliveryman. You are a very naughty cat. I will have to throw you outside."

Tanya bent down and picked up the cat. It felt cold, and it was so thin!

I can't put it outside. It might die, she thought.

"OK. You win," she told the cat. She put the cat on the floor and gave it some milk in a small bowl, and a piece of the salmon from the restaurant. Tanya sat and watched while the cat ate and drank everything. Then the cat came and pushed against her leg. "You want more?" asked Tanya. "I don't know if that is a good idea. It might make you sick."

She gave the cat a little more. Then the cat walked out of the kitchen. "Where are you going? Are you leaving now? That would be good!"

Tanya followed the cat. It walked into the living room and lay down in front of the heater.

"Do you think this is a hotel?" she asked the cat. Of course the cat didn't answer. Even if it could speak, it wouldn't have answered. It was asleep.

Tanya didn't have to go to work the next morning. When she got up, the cat came to the kitchen and sat on the floor next to the refrigerator.

"Good morning," said Tanya to the cat. "Would you like breakfast now?"

The cat had eaten all the salmon the night before. Tanya gave it some milk and cereal. "Try that. It's not as good as salmon, but it's all I have to give you."

Tanya sat at the table and watched the cat.

It's nice to have company, she thought. *It's nice to have someone, well something, to talk to. But I can't keep it. If I lose this apartment, I will never be able to afford another one. I will take it to the animal shelter. People often go there to find a free pet. Maybe someone is looking for a small cheeky cat. I'll wash it, and make it look pretty. Then there will be more chance that someone will want it.*

After breakfast, Tanya took the cat to the bathroom and brushed its fur. The cat was wearing a collar. Tanya took it off and put it on the edge of the bath. Then she tried washing the cat. It was very difficult. There was water everywhere, and Tanya got scratches on her hands and arms. She wrapped the cat in a towel and took it to the living room. The cat lay in front of the heater. Tanya cleaned up all the water in the bathroom. She picked up the collar, and went to the kitchen to make herself a cup of coffee.

She washed the collar and looked at it. It was very pretty. It was purple. There was a silver plate on one side that said 'Princess'. In the middle of the collar was a fake diamond.

When she finished her coffee, Tanya took the collar to the living room. The cat was dry. Its fur was white and fluffy. She put the collar back on the cat.

"So your name is Princess," said Tanya. "And you are a very pretty Persian cat. I guess you were someone's pet. I will tell the people at the animal shelter. Maybe someone is looking for you. I can't take you now. I have to go to work soon, but I have enough time to run to the shop at the corner and buy you some cat food and kitty litter. I'll take you to the shelter tomorrow morning."

Tanya went to the corner shop and came back with the food and the kitty litter.

"Don't make any noise!" she told the cat. "If anyone hears you, they might tell the landlord, and I will lose this apartment. Be a good cat please!"

In the afternoon, the sun came out. The weather was still cold but the winter sun streamed into Tanya's living room. The cat climbed onto the back of the sofa and lay on the windowsill.

The cat watched the cars and people on the street.

There was a traffic jam and all the cars were stopped. Bander Osmore was angry. He was stuck in his car. He couldn't go forwards or backwards. Usually he was a patient person, but he was on his way to visit his grandmother.

She's so upset since she lost her cat, he thought. *Every little thing makes her mad. I told her I would be there at three o'clock to take her to the animal shelter, but I'm going to be very late. I don't know why she thinks Princess will be at the animal shelter. It's a crazy idea but I have to do what she asks. She loved Princess so much and she is so lonely without her.*

Calm down, Bander told himself. *Relax. You can't do anything. The sun is shining. Enjoy it.*

He looked up at the sky. He couldn't see much sky, but then, he saw something that surprised him very much. He was stopped outside an apartment block. The apartments on the second floor had big windows facing the street, and in one of the windows he could see his grandmother's cat.

That's Princess. I'm sure of it! That purple collar looks the same as the one Princess wears, he thought.

The cat moved its head and the sun ray caught the shiny stone in the middle of the collar. Now Bander was sure. It must be Princess. Same colour, same size, and a purple collar with a diamond in it!

Bander took out his mobile phone and started making calls.

When Tanya got home from work, there were two policemen standing outside her apartment.

"Do you live in this apartment?" asked one of the policemen.

"Yes, I do," answered Tanya.

"Please open the door and let us go into your apartment. We believe you have stolen a valuable pet. We believe you are hiding the pet in your apartment," said the other policeman.

Tanya opened the door, and the policemen went in. Tanya followed them. The cat came running out of the living room, and pushed herself against Tanya's legs. One of the policemen picked the cat up and looked at it. He took out his phone and made a call.

"Yes, we have found the stolen cat. White female Persian cat. Purple collar with a diamond and a name plate saying 'Princess'."

The policeman turned to Tanya. "You stole this cat two weeks ago. You will have to come to the police station with us. You are in a lot of trouble."

"No, no!" said Tanya. "That's not true. This cat followed me home last night. It was hungry and dirty. I fed it and washed it. Tomorrow I'm going to take it to the animal shelter."

The other policemen laughed. "I don't believe you! This is not an ordinary cat. The diamond in the collar is worth $100,000. And you stole it!"

"Diamond?" Tanya felt sick. "I thought it was glass."

The first policeman's phone rang. He answered the call. Then he said, "The owner of the cat wants it back immediately. The owner is very old and sick. She is very upset, so the boss said it was OK. We will wait here. Someone is coming to get the cat. Then we will arrest this young woman and take her to the police station."

Tanya put her bag down and started taking off her coat.

"Don't bother taking off your coat," said the second policeman. "We will be leaving here soon."

Tanya wanted to cry. She was in terrible trouble and it wasn't her fault. She hadn't done anything wrong.

She went into the living room and sat on the sofa. The cat sat next to her. The policemen stood at the door and watched them.

About ten minutes later a man came running up the stairs. He spoke to the policeman. Tanya couldn't hear what he said, but he came into the room and picked up the cat.

"Princess! Grandma will be so pleased to see you!"

"This is the woman who stole the cat," said one of the policemen. "We will arrest her."

"No! I didn't!" Tanya was frightened. No one believed her. "I work in a restaurant. The first time I saw this cat was last night. She followed me home. I tried to keep her out of the apartment, but she got in. It was so cold, and she was so thin, I thought she might die outside. So I kept her in here."

Bander looked at Tanya. "I believe her," he said. "Maybe my grandmother's cat just ran away. Or maybe someone stole it. But I don't think it was this woman. When I saw Princess in the window, I had to call the police, so that I could get inside and check if it was really her. But I never said anything about arresting people."

Tanya looked at Bander. He was very handsome and he had a beautiful smile.

"Thank you," she said. "Truly, I didn't take the cat and I didn't plan to keep it. I'm not allowed to have pets in this apartment."

"It's OK," smiled Bander. "My grandmother will be happy to get Princess back. And she should thank you for rescuing her cat."

"What about the diamond?" asked the second policeman. "Even if she didn't steal the cat, she was going to keep the diamond."

"I didn't know it was a diamond," said Tanya. "I thought it was glass. Who puts a big, expensive diamond in a cat collar?"

Bander laughed. "I agree. Only someone as crazy and as rich as my grandmother would do that."

Finally, the policemen agreed to go away. Bander was still holding Princess. "What's your name?" he asked Tanya.

"Tanya."

"That's a pretty name. I'm Bander. I must take Princess back to my grandmother. Please come with me. I know she will want to say, 'thank you'. And then, can I take you out for dinner?"

A little more than a year later, on February 13, Tanya graduated from cooking school. Her parents came from Florida for the ceremony, and Bander was there too. Tanya and Bander had been dating since the first night they met. After the ceremony, Tanya's parents went back to Florida. Bander drove them to the airport. Tanya and Bander waited until her parents went into the departure lounge, and then they walked back to the car. Bander sat behind the wheel, but he didn't start the engine.

"Why aren't we moving?" asked Tanya. "Is something wrong?"

"No. I have a present for you. It's a graduation present and a Valentine's Day present."

"I forgot tomorrow was Valentine's Day," laughed Tanya.

Bander reached over to the back seat of the car. He handed Tanya a big box. "Open it," he said. "I hope you will like it."

Tanya opened the box and looked inside.

"Oh!" she said.

Inside the box was a kitten. A very pretty grey Persian kitten.

"Her name is Azita. Azita was a Persian princess," said Bander.

Tanya picked up the kitten. She was soft and cute.

"Do you like her?' asked Bander.

"She's gorgeous! But Bander, I can't have a kitten. You know my apartment rule is 'no pets'."

"Uh, yes. I do know that. But… but she has a collar. Please look."

Tanya held the kitten up. The collar was pink but the kitten was so fluffy it was difficult to see it. A piece of ribbon was tied around the collar, and hanging from the ribbon was a ring.

Bander looked nervous. "It's an engagement ring. I didn't know how to propose to you. Then I remembered how we first met."

Tanya kissed Bander. "I would love to marry you. But are you allowed pets in your apartment?"

"The truth is, no. I can't have pets either. But my grandmother said if you agree to marry me, we can have the apartment upstairs from her. She owns the building, so of course the rule is no dogs, but cats are very welcome!"

THANK YOU

Thank you for reading Be My Valentine. (Word count: 9,013) We hope you enjoyed the stories.

If you would like to read more graded readers, please visit our website http://www.italkyoutalk.com

Other Level 3 graded readers include
A Dangerous Weekend
A Holiday to Remember
Akiko and Amy Part 1
Akiko and Amy Part 2
Akiko and Amy Part 3
Different Seas
Enjoy Your Business Trip
Enjoy Your Homestay
I Need a Friend
Old Jack's Ghost Stories from England (1)
Old Jack's Ghost Stories from England (2)
Old Jack's Ghost Stories from Ireland
Old Jack's Ghost Stories from Japan
Old Jack's Ghost Stories from Scotland
Old Jack's Ghost Stories from Wales
Party Time!
Stories for Christmas
The Curse

Together Again
Who is Holly?

ABOUT THE AUTHOR

I Talk You Talk Press is a Japan-based publisher of language textbooks, graded readers and language learning/teaching resources.

Our team is made up of highly experienced language teachers and translators, who have all studied at least one additional language to an advanced level.

This experience enables us to design our materials from the perspective of both the teacher and the learner. We consult with both teachers and language learners when designing our textbooks and graded readers, and test our materials extensively in the classroom before publication.

We are a fast-growing press, and currently publish graded readers for learners of English. We publish new graded readers monthly.

www.ingramcontent.com/pod-product-compliance
Lightning Source LLC
Chambersburg PA
CBHW022349040426
42449CB00006B/792